GEARED FOR GROWTH BIBLE STUDIES

DISCOVERING GOD'S GLORY

WHAT GOD IS REALLY LIKE

BIBLE STUDIES TO IMPACT THE LIVES OF ORDINARY PEOPLE

The Word Worldwide

Written by Leah Cubit

reaching the unreached

CHRISTIAN
FOCUS

Contents

INTRODUCTORY STUDY

What is Glory? Where do we see it? In ourselves? In every day life? Describe the greatest exhibition of glory you have ever seen. What is glory? Glory is the display of honour, goodness, power, authority, capacity, character and beauty of the one displaying it. The coronation of Queen Elizabeth II was the supreme display of her glory. In our day, the city's hosting of the Olympic Games is its glory, the announcement of victory and the presentation of a medal is a champion's glory.

What is God's Glory? It is all of the above so let us consider how each of these facets of God's Glory has been manifested, either in Bible history, in secular history, or in our experience today. Let us glance briefly at some manifestations of God's Glory as we see it in Scripture. As we read, we will see how those who saw it responded:

Abraham: *Acts 7:2-4* The God of Glory appeared and said...
We are not told how God appeared to him. Was it in a dream, an angel, a blinding light? We do not know, but it was so overwhelming that Abraham obeyed. When he went out from Ur, he did not know where he was going, but he did know the One who had told him to go. History was made! What would history have been if Abraham had not obeyed?

Moses: *Exodus 3:2-6.*
This was no ordinary fire. This was God's revelation to speak to Moses. How did this manifestation of God affect Moses? Not only did it affect him on that day, but his whole life was changed. He gave up caring for sheep to lead three and a half million slaves out from their taskmasters, through forty years of desert life, toward the land promised to them by God. And all through those experiences he proved the power, the presence and the constant comfort of God Who had appeared to him in the burning bush.

Isaiah: *Isaiah 6:1-5, 8.*
Isaiah saw the Glory of God. Yes, he was devastated, melted by the realisation of his own unworthiness before that great eternal, almighty, glorious God. He was cleansed and empowered to be sent on a life-long and very difficult ministry. From this he saw very little fruit, but what a rich treasury of writings he has left for God's people these past two and a half thousand years!

Ezekiel: *Ezekiel. 1:1, 25-28; 2:1, 2; 3:22-24.*
Ezekiel's visions were spectacular and indescribable. All he could do was to fall face down. In seeking to describe it, (Ezek. 1:28), he did not say, 'This was the glory of the Lord,' but 'There was the *appearance* of the *likeness* of the glory of the Lord'. No words were adequate to clearly express what he saw. His ministry involved many symbolical and painful acts portraying God's word and His purposes. His life was a life of sorrow but of obedience.

Paul: *Acts 9:3-6, 17-20.*
History was changed! How was history changed because Paul saw the glory of the Lord? All of these instances were spectacular revelations, supernatural. But if we look around us, we see the Glory of God in many ways. The beauty of God is revealed in nature, in His strength, His authority, His wisdom, the history of His church. Let us consider for a moment some of these things, and worship Him; 'who revealed Himself to us'.

The Glory of God...
Is His Creation. *Psalm 8*
Do we see the glory of God as the writer did and would we react the same?

Is His Authority and Power. *Exodus 3:7, 8, 19-20; 4:2-4, 6-7; Isaiah 30:30.*
God's glorious voice is heard in the elements.

Is His Character or Attributes. *Exodus 34:5, 6; Psalm 145:9, 13, 15-17.*
What things do we find out about the character of God in these verses?

Is His Supremacy, His Splendour. *Psalm 145:1-5; Psalm 104:1-4; 1 Chronicles 16:23-29.*
Notice what we read in these verses of God's greatness, mighty acts, and the glorious splendour of His majesty.

Is His Incomprehensible Wisdom in redeeming mankind from sin
When Adam sinned God called out, 'Where are you?' From the beginning He wanted reconciliation of man with Himself, that personal relationship restored. He killed an animal as a substitute sacrifice for Adam's sin. Then He instituted animal sacrifices as sin offerings. These covered men's sins over the long period before God sent His Son to be the perfect sin offering to redeem us back to Himself. Galatians 4:4-7.

Is Jesus Christ Himself. *John 1:14, 18; Hebrews 1:1-4.*
This tremendous subject will be dealt with in Studies 8, 9 and 10.

Is His Church. *Ephesians 5:25-27*
The Church of God, His people born of the Spirit of God and joined together by that Spirit, has existed down through the ages in spite of persecution, attempts to annihilate it, false doctrines, upsurge of satanic religions, cults, materialism – but God and His church continues to progress. And it will yet be revealed as a glorious church, without spot and wrinkle, glorified, and bringing more glory to God throughout endless ages.

Where does the majesty of God begin? What are the limits of His glory? How can we comprehend Him? Let us ask God to enlighten the eyes of our understanding and enlarge our hearts as we continue these studies.

STUDY 1

...IS HIS CREATION

QUESTIONS

DAY 1 *Genesis 1:1; Psalm 19:1-6.*
a) What a majestic statement is *Genesis 1:1!* Divide this verse into four phrases and make a statement about each one.

b) In what way do they do this? *Psalm 19:1, 2.*

DAY 2 *Psalm 148*
a) Name some things God has created: in the spiritual heavens; in the heavens of outer space; in the skies; in the formation of the earth; creatures.

b) How is God's splendour described?
Let us take a moment to do what this Psalm tells us.

DAY 3 *Psalm 8:1-9; Genesis 1:26, 28, 29.*
a) What exalted position has God given man?

b) What are the implications of man having this status?

DAY 4 *Job 37:2-13*
a) Man has been given dominion over the earth, but what things stated here can he NOT control?

b) State some reasons God sends so-called disasters *Job 37:7, 13.*

DAY 5 *Job 38:4-38*
a) What would you say if God said these words to you personally?

b) How would *Romans 11:33-36* be a help?

DAY 6 *Job 39:13-30*
a) What evidences of life do we read of in these verses?

b) Discuss: what is life?...and what is the difference between the life of an animal and that of a human? *Genesis 1:20, 24, 26; 2:7* may help.

DAY 7 *Job 42:1-6; Psalm 8:1-9; Ephesians 1:17, 18.*
There is great spiritual value in observing God's creation and knowing Him better. What is it?

NOTES

'In the beginning GOD' – God always existed. Our minds cannot stretch to comprehend this – we just BELIEVE it. That is the essence of faith. Faith is being sure of what we do not see (Heb. 11:1). We can imagine a beginning, but we cannot comprehend a 'before the beginning'. But we know that before that beginning there was supremely God. John 1:1 says, *'In the beginning was the Word, and the Word was with God, and the Word was GOD.'* The Word was the thought, the mind, even when unspoken. That thought and mind was and is personality, the great emotional, personal intelligence who created all things, upholds all things, and is all wisdom, power, love, mercy, compassion and justice.

In the beginning was God, who began creation with a purpose – to glorify Himself. To glorify Himself was not sinful, because He knew that He Himself is all purity, utter holiness, magnificent beauty, and whoever of His creation saw that wholeness of glory would himself be edified, would reflect that glory, and would himself be glorified. Most of the glory of God would centre around:

His person – Who He is and what He is like; His creation and His relationship with His people.

God created all things, giving life to animals and plants. Then He made man in His own image, breathing into him His own life. Man was thus a spiritual being, able to understand God and spiritual things, able to make choices even about his eternal destiny. God made man to be ruler over the earth and its living creatures and plant life. This was and still is a sacred responsibility – to care for and further to beautify the earth, and to use it for his needs. But man has somewhat perverted his role. 'The sacred cow' of India makes the cow ruler and the man as servant. 'Save the snails', if ignoring man's needs, makes the snail the ruler. 'The tree my brother' makes the tree equal to the ruler. As rulers, we must rule with God's wisdom, justice, discretion and love.

What would we say if God spoke personally to us as He spoke to Job concerning all of the grandeur of His works? 'Majesty! Worship His majesty!', 'Holy, Holy, Holy is the Lord God Almighty', 'I am a worm, and no man', 'I despise myself, and repent in dust and ashes', have been some of the responses to the revelations of God.

It would be a good spiritual exercise to read slowly before the Lord the whole passage from Job 36:22 to 42:6. Perhaps you might also make a bookmark list so that you can turn often to read Psalms that speak of His creation and greatness. See Psalms 8, 29, 33, 46, 93, 97, 99, 104, 145, 148, 150. You will be blessed.

God gave life. *'In Him was life, and the life was the light of men.'* John 1:4.

STUDY 2
...IS THE SPLENDOUR OF HIS NAME

QUESTIONS

DAY 1 ELOHIM; EL-SHADDAI *Genesis. 1:1; 17:1.*
Identify in these passages the different Names given to God. If you have a Bible Dictionary try to find out the meanings of these Names. (see Notes for Day 1).

DAY 2 *Exodus 3:1-5.*
a) Who was it that appeared to Moses in the bush? Verse 2, 4?

b) What was the significance of the bush not burning up?

c) Can you get a clue from verse 14? – or from *Psalm 90:2?*

DAY 3 *Exodus 3:5-12.*
a) How did God identify Himself to Moses? *verse 6.*

b) Who was to bring the Israelites out of Egypt? *Exodus 3:8, 10, 12.*

DAY 4 I AM THAT I AM – JEHOVAH *Exodus 3:13-15.*
Moses learned that day the real meaning of a wonderful name of God. What was that name? Find out what you can of the meaning of this Name. (see notes for day 1.)

DAY 5 *John 8:19, 23-24, 28, 57-59.*
a) Why did Jesus say in *verse 58* "I am" rather than "I was"?

b) Why did the Jews attempt to stone Him?

DAY 6 *Genesis 1:1; Exodus 3:14; Psalm 20:1, 7; Exodus 34:5-7.*
What do you find out about God in each of these verses?

DAY 7 ALPHA AND OMEGA *Revelation 1:8, 17, 18; 22:12, 13.*
a) The Name given to the Lord God is ...

b) The Name given to the Lord Jesus is ...

c) We learn from this that ...

NOTES

Elohim. El alone means God or god – mighty one or strong one.

In Genesis 1:1 we find that the name for God is not El, but Elohim, a word indicating plurality in unity. It is something like our word 'cluster' or 'crowd'. Like those words too Elohim takes a singular verb, and singular adjectives and pronouns as well. "I (singular) am Elohim (plurality in unity), and there is no Elohim beside Me." (Deut. 32:39). But this same Elohim can also use the plural, as in Genesis 1:26, "Let us make man in our image." This plurality means God is not confined as He would be if He were just one – He has the ability in Himself to represent Himself in different ways and in different persons. Indeed He has done this, as we know, in manifesting Himself as Father, Son, and Holy Spirit – all one God.

El-Shaddai. In Genesis 17:1 God reveals Himself as "God Almighty", the all-sufficient one, complete, nothing lacking. El means God, the strong one. 'Shaddai' is related to the word 'mother' or 'breasted one,' thus revealing God as the father-mother God, the one who pours His life in to His children, who nourishes, satisfies, strengthens, and makes them fruitful. What an encouragement this must have been to Abraham, the 99-year-old who didn't yet have any children!

Jehovah. The fire that Moses saw did not consume the bush and die out. Why? Because the fire was the manifestation of the great Holy God. Then God revealed to Moses His most sacred name, "I am who I am," that is, the eternal self-existent One, the One Who has no beginning and no ending, This Name, 'I am, or Jehovah', is also related to the word 'to be', 'to exist', 'life'. 'I am' could just as well be rendered 'I will be what I will be', possessing essential life, permanent existence, infinity of character, personality, being. In Isaiah 43:10, 11 we read, …"I am He. Before me no god (El) was formed, nor will there be one after me. I, even I, am the Lord (Jehovah), and apart from me there is no Saviour." That indeed is the name God gave to Moses to give to the children of Israel – 'I am', present continuous tense, source of life, continuing on throughout eternity, utterly dependable, utterly faithful.

This was the most personal and intimate name of God in the Old Testament. It was made up in Hebrew of the consonants YHWH, the early Hebrew writing not having any vowels. It was such a sacred Name that Jews would not pronounce it, and so the correct pronunciation has been lost. It is thought to have been Yahweh. Because of the interchange of consonants Y with J and W with V in languages, this word Yahweh developed to 'Jehovah'. We should not use this word lightly, not even in the term Jehovah's Witnesses. Let's just call them JWs. It is usually translated Lord in our English versions. Moses constantly used this name, the Lord. It reminded him and the Israelites of the mightiness of the one who had called him, who was leading them out of Egypt, was overcoming Pharaoh, was going before them, giving them laws to obey, taking them into the Promised Land. Theirs was a God above all the gods of Egypt, and over all the obstacles in the way.

In reminding Moses that He was the God of Abraham, He was telling them that He would be to them what He was to Abraham. He would be faithful to His promises, be a guide, a shield, be their sufficiency and their reward.

Jehovah is the eternal, self-existent, personal, utterly dependable one. Knowing this, we will perhaps understand a little of how the Jews felt when Jesus declared, *"Before Abraham was born I am!" (John 8:58).* Here was a man wrapped up in a Jewish body like theirs, having been taught in the scriptures as they had been, and He was claiming to be Jehovah of all their history! Of course they would want to stone Him! Yet that was just what our Lord Jesus was – the Jehovah of all the Old Testament and its history, as subsequent events – His death, burial, resurrection, and ascension – proved.

Alpha and Omega. These references in Revelation ... What name is given to the Lord God? What names are given to the Lord Jesus Christ? What is our response to this? Let us bow down and worship as we consider Him, our eternal, self-existent, almighty God in the person of our Lord Jesus Christ, the Alpha and the Omega, the first and the last.

We will learn more about the names of God in Study 7.

STUDY 3

...IS HIS PRESENCE

QUESTIONS

DAY 1 *Exodus 33:7-11.*
    a) Why did the people look so intently at Moses?

    b) What remarkable things happened as Moses met with God?

    c) Why, do you think, young Joshua did not leave the tent?

DAY 2 *Exodus 33:12-17.*
    If you have an Amplified Bible look up *verse 13* in it.
    a) Compare the way Moses prayed here to the way we pray.

    b) What were his concerns?

    c) Moses wanted God's people to be 'distinguished' from all other people. What would distinguish them?

DAY 3 *Exodus 33:18-23.*
    a) Moses became bolder. His second request was....

    b) What two things did God say He would reveal to Him?

    c) What would He NOT show to him? Why not?

DAY 4 *Exodus 34:5-8; Psalm 103:7-14.*
Compare 33:18 and 19a with 34:5, and then identify each of the things told us in 34:6, 7.
a) What do we deduce from this?

b) What does the word LORD, (Jehovah) mean?

c) Name the added characteristics of God revealed here.

DAY 5 *Exodus 34:8, 9; Isaiah 6:1, 5; Revelation 1:12-17.*
How did these men react to seeing the Glory of God?
a) Moses

b) Isaiah

c) John

DAY 6 *Exodus 33:11, 13, 18-23; 34:5-8.*
Consider what impact this would have made on Moses for the rest of his life.

DAY 7 *Exodus 34:29-35.*
a) What physical effect did the meeting with God have on Moses? God had previously revealed His glory *to* people, but never before *through* them.

b) How does He manifest His glory through people now? See *2 Corinthians 3:18.*

NOTES

There are many aspects of God's glory and He has revealed Himself in many different ways. No man can see God in all of His majestic fullness and live, and so He shows only a part of Himself at any one time.

In this study we have seen the awe that was created by the physical manifestation of God as Moses went into the tent of meeting. Exodus 33:9, 10. The people knew God was there, and they worshipped. Joshua, it seems, could not bear to go out and leave the presence of God. Nothing else mattered! Perhaps this was part of his preparation for his later succession to Moses.

Verse 13 in the Amplified Version reads: " ... *Show me Your way, that I may know You (progressively become more deeply and intimately acquainted with You, perceiving and recognising and understanding more strongly and clearly), that I may find favour in Your sight.*" Can we make this our own personal desire and aim?

What a wonderful, intimate conversation between Moses and God (Exod. 33:12-23)! Do we *converse* with God, expecting Him to answer us as we discuss things with Him?

Psalm 103:7 says: *'He made known His ways to Moses, His deeds to the people of Israel'*. Moses asked to know God's ways, the purposes and reasons behind His deeds. To those of lesser understanding God showed His wonderful deeds – all those miracles in Egypt, through the Red Sea, then the manna and water from the rock in the wilderness. But Moses wanted to know more. What were his purposes behind it all? Where was he going, and where was he leading? God's reply was *"Don't worry. I am with you."* But as we read in Psalm 103:7, He did show Moses His ways. Isn't it wonderful that Moses was there on the Mount of Transfiguration with Jesus discussing His coming death! When did God show Moses about that!? Was it in the grand pattern of the Tabernacle and its structure and rituals of sacrifices – was it the way mankind was to be reconciled to God? All pointed forward to Christ's death. Moses must have understood and was able to discuss it with Jesus there on the Mount. God had shown him His way and His purpose behind all the journeying from Egypt to the Promised Land.

In the affairs of life, in great joy or in sudden tragedy or endless trial we see God's 'deeds'. Maybe as we lie in utter desolation before Him we may ask 'Why?' Then He may remind us of the time that we prayed, 'Lord, draw me closer to You.' Then He may quietly show us that yes, these are His 'deeds', but they are also His 'ways' of drawing us closer to Him, answering our prayer.

Moses' second request was 'Show me your glory'. Did he understand what He was asking? God said, "No man can see Me and live," yet He had spoken to him as a man speaks with his friend. God is light. We may gaze at the light of a candle, even look at a one-hundred watt bulb but it is difficult and dangerous to look directly at the sun. What about a sun one hundred times brighter than our sun? But God's light is greater than that. God reveals only as much light as we are able to bear at specific times in our lives.

Moses asked to see God's glory, and God revealed to him His name! Consider again all of those positive attributes of God in Exodus 34:6-7. The apparent negative attribute – He does not leave the guilty unpunished – is not negative but another positive attribute, it reveals His justice. He is holy, and sin must be punished. Even those of the third and fourth generation who have inherited their parents' vices have opportunities to receive His gift of love, grace and forgiveness. It is lovingly held out to them.

Moses' reaction to this revelation of God was that he 'bowed to the ground and worshipped.' He also recognised in the light of God's holiness the sin of all Israel and their need of forgiveness. Is not this always the reaction of one meeting with a Holy God? Isaiah said, 'Woe to me, I am ruined. For I am a man of unclean lips … ' John the apostle fell at His feet as though dead. Others had similar experiences.

Would Moses, and would the people of Israel ever forget this meeting with God? The rest of Moses' life was to be coloured by the memory of this awesome meeting. Is this why he had confidence to go to God and seek His counsel? Is this why it was said of him that he was more humble than anyone else on the face of the earth? (Num. 12:3).

Let us recall intimate meetings we have had with God, meetings that have changed us, have given us greater understanding of Him, and have perhaps transformed our lives. Let us diligently seek to have more such meetings with Him.

STUDY 4
...IS THE MAJESTY OF HIS PERSON

QUESTIONS

DAY 1 *Exodus 19:9-15.*
a) Why did God want to reveal Himself to the people?

b) What preparations did the people have to make, and why do you think they had to make them?

DAY 2 *Exodus 19:16-22; Hebrews 12:18-21.*
a) God must have had a reason for all of this majestic demonstration. What do you think it was?

b) How did the people react? – and Moses himself?

c) Moses' leadership and authority are indicated in which verses?

DAY 3 *Exodus 40:33-38; John 16:13, 14.*
a) Why could Moses not go in to the tabernacle?

b) Who decided when the people of Israel should move?

c) When we make decisions do we then ask God to bless them, or do we ask Him to direct us and lead us to where He wants us to go?

DAY 4 *Isaiah 6:1-5.*

    a) What enhanced understanding of God would Isaiah have from the things he saw in *verses 1-3?*

    b) Uzziah was a godly and powerful king. What was the significance of the timing of Isaiah's vision?

DAY 5 *Isaiah 6:5-8.*

    What was the effect on Isaiah of seeing the Glory of the Lord?

DAY 6 *Psalm 18:4-19, 46-49.*

    a) What was the Psalmist's situation, and what did he do about it?

    b) Note those beautiful and mighty responses to His child's cry of *verse 6, verses 6, 9, 13, 16a, 16b, 17, 19a, 19b.*

DAY 7 *2 Chronicles 5:4-8, 13, 14; 7:1-5.*

    a) When the glory of the Lord filled the temple what effect did it have on (1) the priests, (2) all the Israelites, (3) the king and the people? Consider *verse 5.* How much was given? Why so much?

    b) What is our motive for Giving. (Personal). Does our giving reflect our appreciation of God? Consider: Is our concept of God too small?

NOTES

As we do these studies, let us take time to linger in the presence of God, to absorb some of His glory and majesty, to allow it to impact on us as it did on those men of long ago. The glory that was on the mountain, that filled the tabernacle and the temple, that same glory that was the cloud which moved to guide the people of Israel, was the very presence of God Himself. Later Hebrew writers called this the 'Shekinah' or 'Shechinah', a very meaningful word to express the visible divine presence.

God was awesome, He was holy, He was frightening, He was powerful and had authority. He could whip up the elements – thunder, lightning, fire, smoke and the mountains, to do His will. He could produce a piercing trumpet sound that terrified the people. When we enter into God's presence today, in our quiet times, or in our church service, do we remember that He is that same awesome God?

Moses had previously entered right into the radiance of the glory of God in the earlier temporary Tent of Meeting and on the mountain; but it had been at the invitation or command of God. When the tabernacle was set up no such invitation was given, and Moses therefore could not go in. We dare not be presumptuous as we approach God. Nadab and Abihu were consumed by fire when they went before the Lord in the wrong way (*Lev. 10:1-3*). What a wonderful privilege we have in that we may approach God through our Lord Jesus Christ at any time! Let us therefore approach Him with understanding and deep reverence. Read Hebrews 10:19-22.

What a celebration as the Ark and all the sacred furnishings were finally put into the magnificent new temple that Solomon had built for the Lord! What praise and shouting and sacrifices! Not quite so conservative in their worship as some of us are! And how does our giving compare?! Do we really know and love God?

Isaiah ministered during the reign of four kings (Isa. 1:1). Yes, he was prophesying during the reign of Uzziah, but after the vision of the Lord, high and lifted up, he was to minister in a new dimension. He was given a difficult and painful assignment – to prophesy, warn and teach a people who would be hard of hearing, unresponsive, and he was to continue over the years until there was nothing left of Israel except broken stumps. It is through a vision that God can show us a task He wants us to do.

Did you enjoy Psalm 18? How God hears the cry of despair of His child! He smashes apart the heavens and reaches down to his aid. He pulls him out of the pit and sets him upon a rock, in the beautiful sunshine of His presence. Have you ever had such an experience?

As the glory and the beauty and the majesty of our God is revealed to us as individuals, let us sincerely pray that He will reveal Himself also to our nation. It would be wonderful for our nation to become aware of God as Israel was when the temple of Solomon was dedicated! Imagine, all the people of the nation praising Him. This is happening in other lands, may it happen here.

STUDY 5

...IS HIS ATTRIBUTES

QUESTIONS

What do we mean by 'Attributes' of God? 'His attributes are what we know to be true of God. They are how God is as He reveals Himself to His creatures.' (A. W. Tozer.)

Incomprehensible. No one can ever fully understand God.

Incomparable. No-one, nothing, can compare with Him.

Holy (perfect) 'The absolute quintessence of moral excellence'(Tozer), utterly separate from anything wrong or unclean.

Omnipotent	All powerful
Omniscient	All-knowing
Omnipresent	Present in all places, everywhere
Sovereign	Absolutely above everything

DAY 1 *Job 36:26; 37:23. Romans 11:33.*
Find five phrases in these verses that show that God is Incomprehensible.

DAY 2 *Leviticus 11:45; 20:8; 1 Peter 1:14-16.*
a) According to these verses What is God like? Choose from the definitions above.

b) What is His command?

c) What is His promise?

DAY 3 *Isaiah 57:15, 18, 19.*
a) What attributes of God do we find here?

b) What are some of His wonderful promises to us?

DAY 4 *Isaiah 40:10-17.*
   a) Note the contrasts in *verses 10 and 11*. What are they?

   b) List other attributes of God that you find in these verses.

DAY 5 *Isaiah 40:22-23, 25-31; Hebrews 1:2-3.*
   a) What is God like according to the verses in *Isaiah*?

   b) What do we learn from the *Hebrews* passage?

DAY 6 *Psalm 139:1-16.*
   Which words listed at the beginning of our questions can you use to describe God in this wonderful Psalm?

DAY 7 *Jude 24, 25; Revelation 4:8, 11.*
   a) What does Jude tell us our God is able to do for us?

   b) What are some of the ascriptions of praise used here that we could use in our worship of Him?

NOTES

This week we have learned a great deal about the Nature of God.

A right concept of God is basic, and yet God is infinite, He is beyond our understanding, past finding out. He is Incomprehensible. And yet in Christ God displays Himself. Read John 1:14, 18 again.

God's Holiness. Here we seek to touch the untouchable, to reach into the unreachable. On glimpsing even a measure of God's holiness men have fallen face down on the ground. *'Woe to me,'* said Isaiah. *'I am ruined...my eyes have seen the King, the Lord Almighty.'* Isaiah 6:5.

We as a people have learned to live with unholiness, and can come nowhere near to grasping the divine, unique, unapproachable holiness of God. He is the 'absolute quintessence of moral excellence, infinitely perfect in righteousness, purity, rectitude and incomprehensible holiness'.(A.W. Tozer). Let us give God time, our most precious commodity, and allow the Holy Spirit to impart to us an understanding of the Holy One. We gain everything and lose nothing by the illumination of God through the Scripture and through His Holy Spirit.

God is...

Omnipotent. What is the most powerful thing you know? A storm at sea? An electrical storm around your house? What is stronger than death? Are we able to escape it? God is all-powerful over all of these.

Omniscient. He knows all things. Read Psalm 139 again and note:
You know me: verse 1-6, 7-12, 13-16a, 16b. When, Wherever, Before, Every day... or Job 38:4, 8, 12, 17? Where, Who, Have you, Have the gates...

Omnipresent. Psalm 139 tells us that too. He is everywhere! If I try to flee to the heavens, to the depths, to the east, to the west, into the darkness, He is there. Yes, even in my mother's womb, He was there, forming me.

Incomparable. Who or what can compare with Him?

Eternal. God is uncreated and is not affected by the changes in what we call 'time'. God can say, *'I am God, and there is no other; ... I make known the end from the beginning, from ancient times, what is still to come. I say: 'My purpose will stand, and I will do all that I please.'* (Isaiah 46:9, 10).

God made us in His own image, to be eternal beings. One may say that death and sin interrupted God's plan, but praise Him, He is omniscient, omnipotent, and sovereign. Because of this, as 2 Timothy 1:10 tells us, *'He has sent Christ Jesus, who has destroyed death, and brought life and immortality to light...'*

How are we able to stand before such a holy God? Read Jude 24, 25 Amplified.

STUDY 6
... IS HIS ATTRIBUTES

QUESTIONS

DAY 1 *James 1:17; Malachi 3:6; 1 Samuel 15:29; Psalm 102:25-27.*
a) From these verses we learn that God is

b) What does the word 'immutable' mean?

DAY 2 *Psalm 97:2; Revelation 15:3, 4.*
a) Put in your own words the meaning of the last half of Psalm. 97:2b; Psalm 119:137; Psalm 145:17.

b) Consider: If 'justice' and 'righteousness' were not attributes of God, what difference would it make to us?

DAY 3 *1 Corinthians 1:9; 10:13; 1 John 1:9; Deuteronomy 32:4; John 14:6.*
a) What are some of the things in which God is faithful?

b) What assurance and comfort do the above verses give to us?

DAY 4 *Jeremiah 31:3, 20; John 7:37; Revelation 22:17.*
Write down some of the words or phrases that illustrate the glory of God's personality.

DAY 5 *Exodus 34:6, 7; Deuteronomy 24:16.*
List some of the aspects of God's character that are the expression of love.

DAY 6 *1 John 4:7-10 , 16.*
a) What is the simple but grand statement about God in these verses?

b) What are some of the bounties we receive because God is love?

c) Discuss: Is true love the basis of other religions e.g. Islam, Buddhism, New Age, Occult?

DAY 7 *Exodus 3:13, 14; Isaiah 6:1-5; Revelation 4:8; John 17:24.*
What wonderful truths do we find in these verses
1) about God?

2) about Jesus' desire for us?

NOTES

God is...

Immutable. There is no mutation, or changing, in Him. Malachi 3:6 says, *'I the LORD, do not change.'* Is God able to change from good to better, or from best to less than the best, from immature to mature, or from one order of being to another? It is unthinkable – He is already perfect, already holy and infinite and so it is impossible for Him to change to anything else. There is no mutation in the moral character of God.

Some may suggest; but we read that God sometimes repents, or changes His plans because of man's prayer or behaviour. Is this contradictory? No, not at all. God has always had within Himself the ability to repent or change direction. In exercising that ability He Himself is not changing. He is putting into action what He IS – sovereign in all situations. We change with history, with experience, for better or for worse, but God is immutable, only good, sovereign. We can rest our faith without any fear whatsoever on Him and Him alone.

Just, Righteous. Can we separate these two words? No, they go together. However, we usually think of justice in relation to law courts, decisions on right or wrong dealings with others, being 'fair'. Notice the ascriptions of praise in heaven given to God by both Old Testament and New Testament saints who had endured affliction. They remembered His marvellous deeds, saying, 'Just and true are your ways,' 'You alone are holy,' 'Your righteous acts have been revealed'. When we get to heaven, all our questions and earthly perplexities will dissolve as we see that God is just – we will acknowledge that what He has done is right.

Faithful. He is absolutely dependable, a 'rock'. Deuteronomy 32:4 says, *'He is the Rock, His works are perfect, and all His ways are just. A faithful God who does no wrong, upright and just is He.'* What better character reference do we need than that? We can rest our whole life here and throughout all eternity on Him.

Love. We have perhaps so grown into our Christian environment that we have largely lost the wonder of this statement. Love is so generous, so outgoing, selfless and concerned. God is love. It is His whole personality. All the attributes of God of which we have learned are emanating from or infused with love. Even His punishing of sin is love. He wishes to purge from His kingdom and His people all that is destructive and that mars His perfect habitation and experience for His people.

Consider the places on earth where there is not that love of God – Islam with its oppression and principle of annihilating all who refuse to come under its rule, heathenism with its blind bondage to idols that people's own hands have made, animism with its never-ending fear of spirits, life-styles of drug-addiction and occultism, where even people's own children are sacrificed in the interests of their bondmasters. What a transformation when God's love is beamed in on their situations! There is light, enlightenment, a whole new world of understanding, cleansing, freedom, life – even the life of God within them, joy in God! 'God is love' – and nothing exceeds the experience of entering into that love. Nothing is sweeter than a personality flooded and overflowing with the love of God.

Sovereign, Almighty, Eternal. Not many of us have had the opportunity of walking in the palace of a King or Queen, seeing the majesty of royalty portrayed in the environs. But here we see the majesty of God revealed in what He Himself is. He is almighty – more powerful than anything we can envisage. He is sovereign – He speaks and it is done. He is eternal – has no beginning and no ending. No human being can create something that is eternal, nor can he have unlimited sovereignty. Yet we are going to see the one who is eternal, and who has that sovereignty! That is why He created us. Furthermore, Jesus has prayed for us, that we should be with Him and see His glory, even the glory that He had with the Father before the foundation of the world, and the glory that He received because He became our lamb, our substitutionary sacrifice for sins. We will see Him seated on the throne in the midst of all of God's holy angels and worshipping saints. God is going to clothe us anew with a spiritual body, make us to understand even as we are now understood by Him. Thus we will not be utterly devastated by the glory of His majesty. In the meantime, let us ponder Him, let us bow and worship as we are able, let us dwell on His attributes, allow the life of God to flow out from us to others and eagerly look forward to His coming.

'The Lord is in his holy temple
let all the earth be silent before him.'

Habakkuk 2:20

There are other Attributes of God not covered in these studies. An excellent book on the subject is, The Knowledge of the Holy, by A. W. Tozer (Harper & Row, Publishers, Inc.)

STUDY 7

...IS HIS NAMES

QUESTIONS

In Study 2 we learned some of the names of God. This week we learn others which reveal more of His attributes or character.

DAY 1 **Adonai** – Sovereign Lord. Master of our lives and of our service. *Genesis 15:1-2.*

a) How did Abraham address God?

b) What was Abraham acknowledging when he called God by this name?

DAY 2 **Jehovah-El Elyon** – Lord God Most High.

Genesis 14:18-20, 22; Psalm 7:17. Some of the pagan gods of that time were called 'god most high'. In what way was Abraham more specific in identifying the true God?

DAY 3 **Jehovah-Jireh** – The Lord Will Provide

Genesis 22:7-14, 17, 18.

a) What did God provide through this incident?

b) Why did He provide these things?

c) Can you recall a time in your life when you made a difficult decision in obedience to God which made a great difference to your life?

DAY 4 Jehovah-Tsidkenu – the Lord our Righteousness
Jeremiah 23:5, 6; 2 Corinthians 5:21; John 12:31; 14:30; John 8:38.
Our first reference is a prophecy about the Messiah who was to come.
How do we know for certain that it refers to Jesus?

DAY 5 Jehovah-M'kaddesh – the Lord Who Sanctifies you.
Leviticus 11:44, 45; 21:8; 20:8.
a) Why should we be holy?

b) Is it possible for us to be holy? If so, how?

DAY 6 Jehovah-Nissi – The Lord is my Banner
Exodus. 17:8-15; Psalm 27:1; Psalm 118:6-12.
a) Often this Exodus passage is used to teach the value of our prayer.
But what was Moses' thought?

b) The Psalmist is safe and certain. In what words does he show us
that the Lord is: 1) Our refuge 2) Our victory?

DAY 7 Jehovah-Rohi – The Lord my Shepherd
Psalm 23; Genesis 48:15; 49:24.
a) What are some similarities between God and a shepherd?

b) Which is your favourite name of God? Why?

NOTES

This week we learn more names of God:

Elohim – the Creator-God, who demonstrates the power and majesty of His being, and who represents Himself as masculine and plurality in unity.

Jehovah – 'I am that I am' – the eternal, self-existent God, used especially as the God of His covenant people, a God of righteousness, holiness, love, and redemption.

El-Shaddai – the mighty, sufficient and satisfying one, the Father-Mother God, Who bestows powers, gifts, blessings and fruitfulness for service.

Alpha and Omega – the beginning and the end, the name that indisputably identifies our Lord Jesus as the God of the Old Testament.

Now for notes on this week's names:

Adonai – Strictly speaking this is a title, as 'sir', 'President', rather than a name. It is translated as Lord (small letters in KJV and as Sovereign in NIV.) The word Adon is the singular, meaning 'master', 'lord' or 'sir'. But when it is used of God it is almost always in the plural! As in the name 'Elohim' this confirms the plurality of God. Adonai signifies the deep caring relationship between the master and his slave bought into his own household – not like the loose relationship with the hired servant.

Jehovah-Jireh – the Lord my Provider. Why would the eternal self-existent one who created all the hosts of heaven and sky and earth test one of His tiny creatures as He tested Abraham? He had given him promises of an inheritance and children numberless as the stars, then made him wait till the extremity of his life to give him an heir and then asked him to sacrifice that heir! God was showing another aspect of Himself to Abraham. He was the provider, even in the most extreme of circumstances. What did He provide? A ram for sacrifice, descendants, salvation for all the nations of the earth! What a God is Jehovah-Jireh! Abraham called the place Jehovah Jireh, vs.14, not only because God 'had' provided, but also because He always 'will' provide.

Jehovah-Tsidkenu – Jehovah our Righteousness. After generations of Israel's spiritual instability and defection from God, Jeremiah prophesied of a 'righteous Branch' and 'King' 'This is the name by which He will be called: Jehovah our Righteousness'. All of scripture portrays the sinfulness of man, Only in Jehovah can man be called righteous. Isaiah 45:24a, 25 says, *"They will say of me, 'In the Lord alone are righteousness and strength'....In the Lord all the descendants of Israel will be found righteous and will exult."* The righteousness of Jehovah our

Righteousness is fully revealed in Jesus. 2 Corinthians 5:21 tells us, *"God made Him who had no sin to be sin for us, so that in Him we might become the righteousness of God."* Do we thank Jesus often enough that He is our 'Tsidkenu'?

Jehovah-M'kaddesh – Jehovah Who Sanctifies. The words 'sanctify' and 'holy' come from the same word root. Sanctification could not appropriately be presented until redemption was fully completed. Leviticus shows how a redeemed people should walk worthy of their calling. This title of God is repeated six times in the two chapters following its first appearance. No other Name more truly expresses the character of Jehovah and His requirements of His people. "You shall be holy, for I Jehovah your God am holy." 1 Peter 2:9 tells us that we are *'a chosen people, a royal priesthood, a holy nation...'* You and I are set apart for God, and in 1 Peter 1:15, *But just as he who called you is holy, so be holy, in all you do; for it is written: "Be holy because I am holy."*

Jehovah-Nissi – Jehovah My Banner. Amalek was Esau's grandson, and his descendants were the number one enemies of Israel. Esau and the Amalekites represented the flesh. As Moses lifted up the rod of God, the banner, symbol of power, the enemy was defeated. Moses called the altar he built 'Jehovah-Nissi' – 'Jehovah Himself is my Banner'. Don't you love those words in Psalm 118:10-12, *'In the name of the Lord I cut them off....in the name of the Lord I cut them off....in the name of the Lord I cut them off!'* The Name of Jehovah was their banner. Now we can withstand our spiritual enemies in the name of our Lord Jesus Christ.

Jehovah-Rohi – The Lord My Shepherd. Perhaps we have thought that Jesus initiated that wonderful picture of the shepherd when He walked this earth. But no, away back in Genesis 48:15 and 49:24 Jacob referred to God as a shepherd. Then David established the name in the well-known Psalm 23, – the almighty, eternal, majestic, sovereign God gently tending His flock, leading, guiding, feeding, protecting, comforting, communicating with them. He was there always, being the strong one in whom they could trust.

There are other names also which we have not considered here, but as we have thought on these names of God, has He become bigger to us? Do we see the glory of His person in the meaning of His names? Is He sufficient for all of our needs? Does He understand our problems? Is He worthy of all our trust, all of our confidence, all of our worship?

Let us therefore spend a few moments in worship of Him.

An excellent book on this subject is (Names of God) by Nathan Stone. (Moody Press.)

STUDY 8

...IS JESUS

QUESTIONS

DAY 1 *John 1:1-5, 14.*
a) What is told us of 'The Word' in these verses?

b) Discuss the meaning of *verses 1-5.*

c) *vs.14* 'dwelling' could as well be translated 'tabernacle'. What are the parallels in this verse and *Exodus 40:34-35?*

DAY 2 *John 1:14, 16-34.*
a) Certain of God's characteristics are identified as being in Christ. What are they?

b) How does John affirm that Jesus is the Messiah?

DAY 3 *Luke 1:30-35.*
a) Identify the Names of God and of the coming Child.

b) Who did Jesus claim to be? *Luke 2:49; John 8:58.*

DAY 4 *Hebrews 1:1-4.*
a) In what words is the glory of the Son declared in these verses?

b) If possible find in your Bible notes or commentary or Bible Dictionary the meaning of the word 'image' as used here.

DAY 5 *Luke 3:21, 22; Matthew 17:1-5; John 12:27, 28.*
a) List the manifestations in these passages of the presence of God.

b) Consider: How would such manifestations have affected us? See *2 Peter 1:16-18.*

DAY 6 *Matthew 16:27; 24:30; 25:31; Luke 21:27.*
What is the common factor in all these verses?

DAY 7 *Luke 24:25, 26; Ephesians 1:22, 23; 3:10, 11.*
What did Jesus mean by the phrase to 'enter His glory'? Let us try to stretch our thinking to comprehend something of what this will mean.

NOTES

Christ has revealed God

Can God be known? In the measure that we are able to comprehend, Christ has revealed Him to us. Let us understand fully the meaning of 2 Corinthians 4:6, *"God … made His light shine in our hearts to give us the light of the knowledge of the glory of God in the face of Christ."* What is the light that God has given to shine in our hearts? His 'own' light – Himself. Why? So that we will know the glory of God. How is that glory of God revealed? In Christ Jesus. So let us allow God to shine into us. Let us recognise that glory of God as we look at our Lord Jesus.

He claims relationship with God – Day 3. Shares in the works of God – Days 1, 4. Shares God's glory and majesty – Days 2, 4, 5. Shares with God in His eternal programme – Day 7.

Christ's glory is in his moral perfection

A brilliant Brahmin scholar wanted to stop the spread of Christianity among his people. He studied the New Testament for eleven years seeking inconsistencies in the life and teachings of Jesus. Not only could he find none, but he became convinced that Jesus was indeed the Son of God.

> 'Jesus was the meeting-place of eternity and time,
> the blending of deity and humanity,
> the junction of heaven and earth.' (J. O. Sanders)

God's glory was manifest in Christ's steadfastness

We see it in His steadfastness, His endurance, His courage and His suffering. Throughout His whole life He showed no fear of disease, demons or men (Mark 5:2-13; John 8:3-11). He was made perfect, mature, by the things which He suffered (Heb. 2:10), not only on the Cross, but throughout His life on earth. He steadfastly set His face to go to Jerusalem (Luke 9:51), knowing full well what awaited Him there. Consider the serenity of Christ as He went under the shadow of that cross looming before Him. "I have eagerly desired to eat this Passover with you," He said to His disciples. "Take, and eat; this is my body…Drink … this is my blood." Then when they had sung a hymn they went out. Can we imagine the angels peering down in wonder seeing the Christ of glory and the glory of Christ as He sang that last Passover hymn (Ps. 115-118) before He was hung on the Cross? Listen – *"This is the day which the Lord hath made; we will rejoice and be glad in it; Bind the sacrifice with cords to the horns of the altar. O give thanks to the Lord, for He is good, for His mercy endureth forever."* (Ps. 118:24, 27, 29). (KJV)

Jesus Created the Church – the Glory of Jesus and the Glory of God

Jesus suffered death, was crucified and for this He has been 'crowned with glory and honour' (Heb. 2:9). Hebrews 12:2 tells us that 'who for the joy set before

Him He endured the cross'. What was that joy that He so looked forward to? Ephesians 1:22, 23; 3:10, 11 reveals to us the whole purpose of the cross – to redeem a people for Himself, to be His body throughout all eternity, that body demonstrating to the principalities and powers, both good and evil the mercy, grace, and 'glory' of God and all of this through Jesus. God manifested His glory in and through and for, Jesus. And then we are astonished to read that 'We ... all reflect the Lord's glory, (and) are being transformed into His likeness with ever-increasing glory' (2 Cor. 3:18)! Yes, it is our conscious or unconscious privilege to reflect to those around us and back to Him His own glory that He has given to us through our Lord Jesus Christ.

> The glory of God is Jesus
> the glory of Jesus is his church
> the glory of the church is the radiance of
> Jesus reflected back to God.

> To God be the Glory, great things He has done,
> So loved He the world that He gave us His Son
> Who yielded His Life an atonement for sin,
> and opened the life-gates that all may go in.

> Praise the Lord! Praise the Lord!
> Let the earth hear His voice.
> Praise the Lord! Praise the Lord!
> Let the people rejoice.
> Oh come to the Father through Jesus the Son,
> and give Him the Glory, great things He has done.
>
> Fanny J Crosby
> Redemption Hymnal No 47.

STUDY 9

... IS THE UNIQUENESS OF HIS SON

QUESTION

Unique: Being without like or equal; alone in kind or excellence.
(The Little Webster Dictionary.)

DAY 1 His birth
Luke 1:35; 2:8-14; Matthew 2:1-2; 2:3, 13; Luke 2:25-32.
One small baby – five unique happenings! What are they?

DAY 2 His relationship with God
Luke 2:49; John 5:19-23; John 17:5.
a) What relationship with God did Jesus always claim?

b) How did He always address Him?

DAY 3 His claims
John 5:24-30; 8:54-58; John 17:4; Revelation 3:20.
Jesus made some astonishing claims. What are they?

DAY 4 His obedience
John 8:28; 12:49-50; 6:38.
a) What words indicate that Jesus never spoke nor acted on His Own initiative?

b) Challenge: Can we for one week seek to emulate Jesus in these two areas? Then for one more...!

DAY 5 His teaching

John 7:37-39; 15:4, 9; 6:51-58; 14:1-6.

a) What, in these verses, sets Jesus out as a unique teacher?

b) Have I claimed these promises for myself? *2 Peter 1:3, 4.*

DAY 6 His death

John 19:23, 24, 28-37.

As found in this passage, in what ways was the death of Jesus like no other death?

DAY 7 His continuing presence

John 14:15-21; 7:37-39.

a) What evidence is there in the first set of verses that the Holy Spirit is the same as Jesus Himself?

b) Say what you think is the meaning of *John 7:37-39.* Does Jesus fit the definition of 'unique' ?

NOTES

Jesus was unique in His... Birth, Relationship with God, Claims, Obedience, Teaching, Death, Continuing presence.

For notes on this lesson I can do no better than to quote most of Dr. Bill Newman's leaflet, *'Jesus Christ, a Fake or for Real'* (Permission obtained.) 'It is a fact of history that Jesus Christ claimed to be God.'

For most of us that is hard to accept. It was also hard for Jesus' contemporaries. Some of them believed Him, some obviously didn't. But they all had to take Him seriously. His capture and execution was a national affair. Within ten years the movement He had started came to the notice of the Roman Emperor, and 2,000 years later His influence, through His followers, is still one of the most powerful forces in the world.

Jesus once challenged His disciples, *"But what about you? Who do you say I am?"* (Matt. 16:15). We also have to answer that question. In order to do so honestly we must give serious attention to what Jesus said and did. .... The implication of Jesus' claim is that God has visited us. His claim to be God must be either true or false. First, consider that His claim was false. Then we have only two possibilities: He either knew that it was false or He didn't.

Was He a liar?

If Jesus knew that He was not God when He made His claim He was lying. If this were so He was also a hypocrite, for He told others to be honest whatever the cost while He Himself was living a colossal lie. More than that, He would also have been a fool, because His claim to be God led to His crucifixion. At His trial the Jewish prosecutor said, 'We have a law, and by that law He ought to die, because He made Himself out to be the Son of God'.

The problem with this conclusion that Jesus was a liar is that it is just not consistent with what we know of His life The man who lived as Jesus lived, taught as Jesus taught and died as Jesus died could not have been a liar.....

Was He mad?

If Jesus thought He was God when He wasn't, then let's face it – He must have had a severe case of psychological maladjustment! Imagine an ordinary man today trying to convince you that your eternal destiny depended on him. You would immediately conclude that he was mad.

But when you examine the historical record of Jesus you find that His life matched His claim.

Consider these facts:
1. He had extraordinary powers to do things that were clearly supernatural.
2. His teaching in the field of ethics and worldview, although 2000 years old, has not been equalled, let alone superseded, despite the tremendous increase in knowledge.
3. We have several descriptions of Jesus being faced by the sceptical 'highbrows' of the day. In each case He exposes the fallacies in their arguments and shows superior intellectual powers. At the same time His life is marked by a calmness, authority and self-possession that makes it impossible to conclude that He was mentally deranged.
4. He proved to be indestructible. You would expect an attempt to kill God would end in failure! When Jesus' enemies succeeded in killing Him they couldn't keep Him dead!

He must be Lord
An unbiased examination of the evidence leads logically to the conclusion that Jesus' claim was true. (end of quotation from Dr. Bill Newman's tract.)

To summarise:
Jesus claims to be God. Either His claims were false or true.
If they were false, He knew His claims were false or He did not know.
If He knew His claims were false He made a deliberate misrepresentation. He was a liar.
If He did not know His claims were false He was sincerely deluded. He was mad.

If His claims were true, He is Lord.
If He is Lord, we can either accept His Lordship or we can reject it.

Jesus is unique!

He is Lord, He is Lord.

STUDY 10
...IS THE CROSS OF CHRIST

QUESTIONS

DAY 1 *1 Corinthians 15:3-5; Acts 4:12; Galatians 6:14.*
a) What were the things that Paul considered of prime importance?

b) Why were they?

DAY 2 *Acts 2:22-24; 3:13-15, 19; 4:10-12; Romans 5:10.*
What was the common theme in all of the N.T. sermons?

DAY 3 *Matthew 26:42; John 19:30; Matthew 28:2, 5, 6.*
The triumph of God is seen in each of these verses. What statements reveal this triumph?

DAY 4 *Hebrews 2:14; 2 Corinthians 5:17-19; Colossians 2:15.*
The glory of God is manifest in five magnificent truths in these verses. What are they?

DAY 5 *Ephesians 1:9, 10; 2:4-6; Jude 24, 25.*
a) The prime purpose of God in all creation was

b) How did He accomplish this?

c) Which part of these verses is most wonderful to you?

DAY 6 *Revelation 5:8-10; Revelation 7:17; 5:6, 11, 12.*
a) Every ethnic group in the world is affected by the death of Christ. How?

b) What is the position or status of the Lamb in eternity?

DAY 7 *Revelation 19:6-8; 21:9, 22, 23; 22:1, 3.*
a) What is the supreme triumph and glory of the cross?

b) What other functions does the Lamb fulfil in eternity?

NOTES

In Study 1 of this series we saw God's glory revealed in His creation, in His mighty acts. The mightiest of all His creation is His creation of the church, for the church is to be His living partner and the manifestation of all that He is and does throughout eternity. The mightiest of His acts was the reconciliation of man to Himself through the death of His Son and His subsequent resurrection from the dead.

We encompass all of this – the death and resurrection of Christ, the cleansing of sin and reconciliation of man back to God – in the simple term, the cross of Christ. In the cross those magnificent attributes of God that we have seen in His names are exemplified and are all brought together in that one act of God at the cross. Let us look at just some of those Names of God again:

Jehovah-Jireh – 'The Lord will provide.' He provided a ram for Abraham to sacrifice instead of his son Isaac. Now Christ is the sacrifice instead of us.

Jehovah – the Eternal 'I Am that I Am'. We learn in John 5:58 that Jesus was the 'I Am'. He died, triumphed over death, to reign eternally as the Lamb slain.

Jehovah-Tsidkenu – 'The Lord our righteousness'. 'God made him, who had no sin be sin for us, so that in him we might become the righteousness of God.' 2 Corinthians 5:21.

Jehovah M'Kaddesh – Jehovah sets His people apart as His Own peculiar people, to holy service. It is through the death of Christ that this is possible.

1 Peter 2:9 says, *"You are a chosen people, a royal priesthood, a holy nation, people belonging to God, that you may declare the praises of him who called you out of darkness into his wonderful light."*

Jehovah-Shammah – 'Jehovah is there'. This is a name we did not look at in our earlier study. It is very meaningful in reference to Christ. Jehovah, the great 'I Am' was there in Christ – in His ministry, on the cross, at the resurrection. He is in us, now, and because of His great work of reconciliation, is 'there', ever present, our all in all throughout eternity.

We read in Colossians 2:9, *'In Christ all the fullness of the Deity lives in bodily form'*. The Godhead was there on the Cross for us! What unfathomable mystery! We can accept it only by faith.

The tabernacle and the Temple rituals looked forward to the Cross, to the Lamb slain Who would not only cover sin but would take it right away, never to be recalled again. Prophets wrote of one who would be pierced for our transgressions, bear our iniquities, pour out his life to death, bear the sin of many, and make intercession for the transgressors (Isa. 53). In John 1:29 he points to Jesus, *"Look, The Lamb of God, Who takes away the sin of the world!*

The Gospel writers, even though Jesus lived for thirty-three years, delegated one third of their narratives to just the last week of His Life and His resurrection. The apostles in their ministry had but one theme – the Cross and its power to reconcile men to God. Likewise the epistles bring us back to this one theme which Paul quoted as being 'of first importance'. (1 Cor. 15:3).

Truly the fulcrum of all of history and eternity is the Cross of Christ. God's purpose in creation was to have a people for Himself, but they sinned, and so could not enter His sinless Glory. Christ redeemed them back to God by His death and the cleansing by His Blood. Yes, the Cross is certainly the centre of time and of eternity.

In the last book of the Bible, Revelation, we see our Lord Jesus exalted throughout as the Lamb, the One slain to purchase men for God from every tribe and language and people and nation. (Rev. 6:8-10). The twenty-seven references to the Lamb in Revelation convince us that we shall see Christ in Heaven always as the Slain One, but glorified! The Lamb, the crucified Jesus, is the Bridegroom of Heaven to Whom the church is to be wedded (19:7-9, 21:9). He, with God Almighty, is the Temple and the Light, and the Throne (21:22-23; 22:1, 3).

The Lamb, the crucified Jesus, the Cross, is the Glory of God throughout eternity. We should say with Paul, *"God forbid that I should glory save in the Cross of our Lord Jesus Christ"* (Gal. 6:14).

> In the Cross of Christ I glory
> Bane and blessing, pain and pleasure,
> towering o'er the wrecks of time.
> by the cross are sanctified.
> All the light of sacred story
> Peace is there that knows no measure,
> gathers round its head sublime.
> joys that through all time abide.
>
> J. Bowring
> Redemption Hymnal No 419

STUDY 11

QUESTIONS

DAY 1 A chosen people
1 Peter 2:9, 10; 2 Peter 1:3, 4.
List the things in these verses that show the uniqueness of God's people and His purpose for us.

DAY 2 A family
John 1:12; Romans 8:14-17; 2 Corinthians 3:17, 18.
a) How do we get into the family?

b) What are some of the privileges of being in it?

DAY 3 A union
John 17:9, 10, 20-26.
List some of the precious truths in these verses and share them.

DAY 4 An enlightened people
2 Corinthians 4:6.
a) What is the light that God has given in our hearts? *John 16:12-15; 1 Corinthians 2:9-14.*

b) Explain as explicitly as you can how men and women may understand the deep things of God.

c) How often do you ask the Holy Spirit to reveal these things as you study His Word and pray?

DAY 5 A body
1 Corinthians 12:27, 12-20; Acts 2:42-47.
a) What are some essential elements in a body?

b) Name characteristics of that first church, or body.

DAY 6 A display
Ephesians 3:10, 11; 2 Corinthians 3:17, 18; Philippians 2:14, 15.
These verses tell us astonishing ways in which the church glorifies
God. What are they?

DAY 7 A testimony
Romans 8:17, 18; 2 Corinthians 4:17, 18; Hebrews 2:10, 11.
a) What two things accompany each other here?

1 Peter 4:12-16; 5:1, 4, 10.
b) What should be our attitude to trials and suffering, and why?

NOTES

I trust we have learned more this week of the 'utter otherness' of the people of God. God is glorified IN us by saving us, separating us out for Himself. He has given a light within us – the knowledge and spiritual understanding of Himself, and indeed that light is Jesus Himself. As we meditate on Him, love Him, live with Him and obey Him, we are transformed from one degree of glory to another – becoming more like Him. There is a uniqueness, a holiness, a quality of life and beauty of character which distinguishes the people of God from those belonging to the world.

We are Chosen. We are 'separate', 'different', 'a holy nation', 'a called people', unique. We have different standards of life from those who do not know Christ, different hopes, spiritual understanding, spiritual wisdom. We have the same ministry that God has – to bring people out of darkness into light, into this unique relationship with the majesty on high. We have the ministry too of demonstrating to principalities and powers in the heavenly places, to angels and demons, the astonishing wisdom and glory of God.

We are Family. We have believed in Christ, we have been born again. The people of the world cannot call our Heavenly majestic God 'Father', but we can. They cannot say they are His children, in union with Him, but we can. Ours is the glorious privilege of being joint/heirs with Christ. This is a reality almost beyond comprehension, nevertheless it is true. As we gaze upon Christ we become like Him. Have you seen an elderly couple who have shared life together become like each other? How often we have seen a family likeness even in an adopted child! What a privilege it is to share the likeness of Christ!

In union with Christ. Let us meditate much on this seventeenth chapter of John. No words are adequate to impart its depth and beauty and wonder. Only the Holy Spirit can enlighten, and as He does we are melted to worship Him, perhaps in utter silence and wonderment. The Psalmist said, "I am a worm, and no man." And yet we are elevated to be sons of the Most High, 'In Christ, and He in us'.

We are the Body of Christ and as such are a community of sharing, caring, worshipping together and witnessing people or we should be! As we manifest the grace of God in our salvation, and the joy and power of God in our daily living we are a display of that grace, power and joy.

A display to whom? To the very real spiritual rulers of darkness, to the heavenly angels, and innumerable host, as we read in Revelation. How then should we live?!

We display the Majesty of God – even as the stars of the universe display the glory of God. Rulers and authorities in Heavenly realms gaze down on the church and marvel at the manifold wisdom of God displayed. They are amazed that His eternal purpose was able to be fulfilled through Christ.

A testimony. There is also a sober fact and a solemn obligation as we live our lives here on earth. The fact is that glory is also associated with suffering. We share in Christ's suffering. John on Patmos (Rev. 1:9) said, *"I, John, your brother and companion in the suffering and kingdom and patient endurance that are ours in Christ Jesus".* Those three things were Christ's portion, and they are ours also – for greater glory. The solemn obligation we have is to minister to others, whatever our situation, in tranquillity and in suffering, in joy or in pain, in light or in darkness. Let us remember and let us testify, God is there. What a privilege is ours to be the recipients of such grace, love and mercy, to be the central purpose of all of God's work and His treasured possession. 1 Peter 1:10-12 tells us that the prophets who prophesied of this salvation of ours searched diligently to try to understand it. It tells us too that *'even angels long to look into these things.'* But God has revealed them to US by His Spirit (1 Cor. 2:10). Do we comprehend that we are in the spotlight of history and eternity? Prophets didn't understand, angels didn't understand. But Jesus said, *"When He, the Spirit of Truth, comes, He will guide you into all truth...He will bring glory to me by taking from what is mine and making it known to you."* John 16:12-14.

Yes, truly we are God's people. Of all of God's creation we are His 'show-window' displaying the magnitude of His wisdom, His love and His glory.

> O the deep, deep love of Jesus!
> Vast, unmeasured, boundless, free;
> Rolling as a mighty ocean
> In its fullness over me.
> Underneath me, all around me,
> Is the current of Thy Love;
> Leading onward, leading homeward,
> To my glorious rest above.
> > S. Trevor Francis
> > Redemption Hymnal No 15

STUDY 12

...IS THE MAJESTY OF OUR FUTURE

QUESTIONS

DAY 1 **In the worship of heaven**
Psalm 93; 2 Chronicles 6:18; Revelation 4:8, 11.
What do we learn here,
    1) about God, and

    2) about His creation?

DAY 2 **In the celebration of redemption**
Revelation 5:5-14.
a) What names are given to Jesus in these verses?

b) Why is the Lamb to be worshipped?

DAY 3 **In the worship of those who have suffered**
Revelation 7:9-17; 1 Peter 4:13.
a) The experiences of these people had been............

b) But they had a deep joy. It was *(vv. 10, 14)* ....

c) How we should pray for people in deep affliction?

DAY 4 **In those who have overcome**
Revelation 12:10, 11; Romans 8:35-39; Revelation 21:1-4, 7.
a) Name some ways in which Satan may accuse us.

b) How are we able to overcome? See also *Hebrews 12:2-3.*

DAY 5 In the Bride of Christ
Revelation 19:6-8; 21:3-7, 22-27.
a) Who is the Bride?

b) There are many positive blessings in those verses in *chapter 21.*
What are your two favourites, and why?

DAY 6 In the life of eternity
1 John 3:2; Revelation 21:22, 23; 22:1, 5.
In that city
a) The temple is ....the light is ....

b) the lamp (light-holder) is ....

c) the river is ....and it comes from ....

d) life expectancy will be ....

DAY 7 In the answer to our Lord's prayer
John 17:1-5, 24; 1 Peter 5:10.
a) Jesus brought glory to God. How?

b) What was His desire for us?

c) We have a wonderful promise and assurance. What is it?

NOTES

What is Heaven like?

Paul says in Philippians 1:21 that 'to die is gain', and that heaven is 'better by far'. What is the best life here on earth that you could desire? House, with scenery, sunshine, travel, freedom, family, friends, security health? Paul says that that other life is 'better by far'. He says again in 2 Corinthians 5:1-4 that if our earthly tent that we live in – our body – is destroyed, we have an eternal house in heaven, not built with human hands..... While we are in this tent – our temporary dwelling-place – we groan and are burdened, wishing to be clothed with our heavenly dwelling – our real home. Then our mortal body will be swallowed up by that which is reality for ever.

In Hebrews 11:8-10, 16 we are told that Abraham looked for 'a better country', better even than the Promised Land for which he had left his magnificent home and his position in Ur. It was a 'new heaven and a new earth'. 2 Peter 3:13.

Paul had a glimpse of heaven. He was caught up into the third Heaven, where he saw inexpressible things, too sacred and too glorious to express in the words of earth. 2 Corinthians 12:1-4. Again we read: *'No eye has seen, no ear has heard, no mind has conceived, what God has prepared for those who love Him'* (1 Cor. 2:9).

What does our entering Heaven mean to Jesus?

Jesus said, *"In my Father's house are many rooms.... I am going there to prepare a place for you"* (John 14:2). He left His Father's glory and came down to live among us, and save us for Himself to be His holy Bride. He is extending that love now as He prepares in utmost detail and care a magnificent permanent home for us! We could never conceive of the majesty and splendour of that home. He prayed (John 17:24), *"Father, I want those you have given me to be with me where I am, and to see my glory, the glory you have given me because you loved me before the creation of the world."* As one after another of us drop off from this life, the Father is answering that prayer of Jesus – those redeemed ones are with Him, seeing His glory.

John further assures us in (1 John 3:2) that *'we shall be like him, for we shall see him as he is'*! What glory, what joy, as our Saviour greets us and introduces us to His and our eternal home. Our 'room' will be a bridal suite, not confined by walls, but extending to infinity.

We are His inheritance! In Ephesians 1:18 Paul says, *"I pray that the eyes of our hearts may be enlightened in order that we might know the riches of His glorious inheritance in the saints!"* Did you know that Jesus has an inheritance – a glorious inheritance – and that that inheritance is US?!! He has given Himself to obtain us. He has given us glory – our salvation, new birth through the Holy Spirit. He has made us to become partakers of the divine nature, has called us out to be a separate people, has made us through His blood and His power to be overcomers. All this reflects to give glory back to Him. It gives Him an inheritance in the saints. It gives Him an eternal companion. That is why in Hebrews 12:2 we read, 'that for the JOY set before Him He endured the cross'. That joy? The prospect of US redeemed, and His for ever.

Will we recognise our loved ones in Heaven?

Friends and loved ones will be there. Saints of old will be there. And we will recognise them. A demonstration of this was given on the Mount of Transfiguration. We do not read that Jesus had to introduce Moses and Elijah to the disciples. They recognised them instantly. Paul was looking forward to meeting his flock. He said, *"What is our hope, our joy, or the crown in which we will glory in the presence of our Lord Jesus Christ when he comes? Is it not you? Indeed you are our glory and joy."* 1 Thessalonians 2:19-21. Yes, he would recognise them and rejoice in them. Those to whom we have ministered Christ will be there. What a meeting, what a greeting! We will meet and recognise godly grandparents who have prayed for us, ministers and Sunday School teachers who cared and prayed for our eternal welfare. Oh, what an opening of the eyes there will be on that day! Let us even now praise and worship our wonderful Lord.

What shall we be doing in Heaven?

We will be living a life of praise and worship. Jesus, throughout the book of Revelation, is referred to as 'the Lamb', and we will forever be aware that it is He who has bought us by His sacrifice. We will realise in a way that we cannot understand now, that He is God, the Alpha and Omega, the first and the last. He is the Jehovah, the I Am that I Am who was revealed to Moses. But for now He shows us that we, His church, are His Bride, and He gives us a glimpse of the marriage feast. But then He closes the door on a future where our understanding can penetrate no more. The wedding is just the beginning of a great relationship, a life together, doing things together, home, fellowship, family. God is a Creator. Is He going to cease to create? What will our life with Him be like in that place where 'Nothing impure will ever enter it' (Rev. 21:27)? All the splendour of the nations brought into it (Rev. 21:24) will be nothing in comparison with the glory and splendour of our great God and of our eternal life with Him.

To Him who is able to do immeasurably more than all we ask or imagine, according to His power that is at work within us, to Him be glory in the church and in Christ Jesus throughout all generations, for ever and ever! Amen. Ephesians 3:20

Answer Guide

The following pages are only a guide to the questions asked and are in no way exhaustive. To get the full benefit from these studies, it is recommended that you answer the questions first before turning to the answer guide. Remember to read through the notes again after completing your study.

INTRODUCTORY STUDY

If Abraham had not obeyed:
We would not have had the nation of Israel – nor the Arabs.
We would not have had a depository for the Laws of God, from which we gain not only our Christian standards of right and wrong, but also our government's basic standard of law and justice.
We would not have the prophets as we know them, nor the history of Israel from which we learn so much.
Where would Jesus have been born?
We could go on, but Abraham did obey God... and so did Moses... and Isaiah, and Ezekiel, and Paul. Why did they obey? Because they saw the majesty, the authority, the power, the glory of the infinite God. There was no alternative for them but to go along in God's plan, to be a part of His eternal programme. How rich were their lives of walking with Him, and how enriched we have been down through the ages!

The Glory of God is His Creation
After the reading of *Psalm 8* you may wish to pause and have a time of worship.

The Glory of God is His Authority and Power
You may wish to discuss the difference between authority and power. e.g. a man has the authority to save a shipload of drowning people, but he does not have the power. Another may have the power to destroy a forest, but he does not have the authority. God has all power and all authority to use as He sees fit. Consider God's glorious voice in the elements – the mighty roll of thunder – who on earth can create this? The display of lightning, the downpour of rain. Who can do it, or who can prevent it?

The Glory of God is His Character, Attributes, or what He is
God is loving, compassionate, faithful, righteous. If anyone questions the 'justice' of God you could take them to Luke 12:47, 48; Rev. 16:5-7.

The Glory of God is His Supremacy, His Splendour
Emphasise the words 'splendour', 'majesty'. Are we passing on to the next generation what we know of God's splendour, majesty, and holiness?

The Glory of God is His Incomprehensible Wisdom in Redeeming mankind from sin.
If appropriate to your group you may want to emphasise this paragraph and use also such verses as Romans 6:23, 2 Corinthians 5:17.

The Glory of God is Jesus Christ Himself
Hebrews 1:1-4. JESUS is the glory of God. In studies 8, 9 and 10 we will see much more of this.

GUIDE TO STUDY 1

DAY 1 a) e.g. 'In the beginning' – when was the beginning? Man cannot comprehend it. 'God created' – only God can create (something out of nothing). 'the Heavens' – birds fly there, the sun and the moon are there, planets of ice or stone or fire or gas are there, galaxies are there. 'the earth' – men spend lifetimes studying soil, the rocks, the water, the air, not to mention all peoples, animals and plants. Why did God make them like that? Colossians 1:16 – for Himself – for His own pleasure – and He has shared them with us!
b) Personal.

DAY 2 a) Angels, heavenly hosts, sun, moon, stars, rain, clouds, lightning, hail, snow, stormy winds, ocean depths, mountains, hills, trees, sea creatures, wild animals, domestic animals, birds, various ages and ranks of mankind.
b) Above the earth and heavens

DAY 3 a) A little lower than the heavenly beings. Ruler over the earth – over animals, birds, plants, fish.
b) He is to use it and care for its contents and creatures as God would.

DAY 4 a) Lightning, thunder, snow, rain showers or downpours, tempests, cold, wind, ice.
b) So that all may know that it is God's work – man cannot control it. To show His Love. Sometimes to punish men.

DAY 5 a) Personal.
b) His wisdom is so much greater than ours.

DAY 6 a) Oxford Dictionary summarised – 'Life is functional activity peculiar to organised matter, especially – animal or plant before death.' Dictionary of Synonyms and Antonyms – 'Life, – existence, animation, vitality, essence, breath...'
b) Of an animal the Bible simply says, 'God said – He created – it was good.' But man was made in His image, formed from the dust of the earth, and most importantly, God breathed his own life into him. He became a living being having a spirit that is able to communicate with God. In this way man is different from all other creation.

DAY 7 We see His glory, and it humbles us. We see His eternal purposes for us. All this 'reduces us to size', makes and keeps us humble before Him, and lifts our hearts in worship to Him.

GUIDE TO STUDY 2

DAY 1 Genesis 1:1 – God. Elohim. El means 'God' or 'god'. The suffix 'him' is the Hebrew ending for all masculine names in the plural.
Genesis 17:1 – God Almighty – El Shaddai.
(You may wish to read paragraphs 1, 2 and 3 of the study notes at this stage).

DAY 2 a) The Lord Himself. Note that in the O.T. when the phrase 'an angel of the Lord' is used it means literally an angel. When 'the angel of the Lord' is used, it is the Lord Himself.
b) God is eternal, does not die.

DAY 3 a) He said that He was the God of Abraham, Isaac, and Jacob.
b) God and Moses together.

DAY 4 I Am Who I Am. (To enlarge on the meaning of this Name, allow time to read now the five paragraphs in the notes allocated to Day 4.)

DAY 5 a) He was not saying primarily that He existed before Abraham, but that He is indeed Jahweh using that greatest, most sacred Name of God.
b) They were appalled at what they thought was the utmost in blasphemy. (Read now the notes for Day 5.)

DAY 6 Genesis 1:1 – God existed before all things. He was creator of all things.
Exodus 3:14 – He is self-existent and everything that He wants to be.
Psalm 20: 1, 7 – He will answer when we call.
His name will protect us. We can trust in His name. (His name is His character.)
Exodus 34:5-7 – His character is in His name. Note that when God said He would show Moses His name, he showed all those characteristics – compassion, graciousness, slowness to get angry, love to 1,000s forgiveness, justice in dealing with rebellion.

DAY 7 a) Alpha and Omega
b) Alpha and Omega, the First and the Last, the Beginning and the End.
c) Jesus and God are one and the same.
(Complete the reading of the notes – Day 7.)

GUIDE TO STUDY 3

DAY 1 a) They revered God, Moses was going right into the very presence of God. They knew that Moses was conversing with God about them and getting His directions concerning them. See John 12:49 and 15:5b.
b) The people worshipped. The cloud lingered. God spoke with Moses as a man speaks with his friend.
c) Joshua lingered in the presence of God, absorbed in worship. How does this speak to us of our prayer times?

DAY 2 a) So often our prayers comprise lists of things we want God to do. Here we see Moses' deepest desire was to grow to know God better...
b) That I may find favour in Your sight.... Emphasise the meaning of the word 'know' in this Amplified version. Is this how we want to know God, to know His ways, to know Him and to find favour with Him? 'Don't send us alone without You, God.'

c) God's presence. Discuss here how very vital it is that we are examples to others. We should have a close relationship with God. Others are affected and influenced. Note in the O.T. how Israel was blessed when they had good Judges or Kings. They turned to evil when their leaders were evil or compromised.

DAY 3 a) That God would show him His glory.
b) His goodness and His name.
c) His face. Nobody could see God's face and live.

DAY 4 a) In respect of Moses' request to see God's glory, He said He would show him His goodness and proclaim His name. Which is what He did. Further to His name He proclaimed His compassion, graciousness reluctance to be angry, love, faithfulness and forgiveness. God's character and glory is wrapped up in His Name.
b) God's character and glory are wrapped up in His name.
c) The eternal self-existent one.

DAY 5 a) Moses bowed to the ground and worshipped.
b) Isaiah – dismayed, with overwhelming sense of sin.
c) John – fell at His feet as though dead.

DAY 6 e.g. He would more deeply understand the majesty of God and His attributes of love and justice. It would keep him humble (Moses was more humble than anyone else on the face of the earth, Num. 12:3).

DAY 7 a) It made his face radiant with the glory of God. (Matthew Henry has a good comment on this.)
b) By the indwelling Holy Spirit reflecting God's glory through His blood bought children.

GUIDE TO STUDY 4

DAY 1 a) So that the people would hear God speaking to Moses and thereafter trust him as their leader.
b) Consecrate themselves for two days, wash their clothes, Moses put limits around the mountains, verse 23, and they were warned not to touch even the foot of it. They were to have no sexual relations.
To impress on them the sacredness and awesomeness of meeting with such a holy God.

DAY 2 a) To show His greatness, holiness, awesomeness.
b) Everyone trembled. Moses also trembled with fear.
c) Exodus 19:17, 19.

DAY 3 a) Because the glory of the Lord filled it.
b) God did.

c) Discuss. Also, if we make our own decisions and ask God to be with us, will He follow us? Will His glory be with us?

DAY 4 a) God was supreme ruler, His presence and glory was everywhere, even angels could not look on His glory. Their feet were covered as a sign of humility. They used only one third of their strength in activity, the other two thirds were in worship.
b) God is utterly holy, and even the world's wickedness will be used to demonstrate His holiness.

DAY 5 He realised his own utter unworthiness and sinfulness as well as the sinfulness of his people. He was willing to go in response to the Lord's appeal. The awesomeness of God's holiness had never left Him, nor the awareness that God was with those of lowly and contrite heart.

DAY 6 a) Psalm 18:4-6a – entangled by cords of death, distress, destruction He cried to the Lord.
b) He.. verse 6 hears my voice, verse 9 parted the heavens and came down, verse 13 thundered from heaven, verse 16a reached down from on high, verse 16b drew me out, verse 17 rescued me, verse 19a brought me out into a spacious place, verse 19b rescued me 'because he delighted in me'! There is much more in this Psalm. Hide it in your treasuries of memory. Well can David, and we, say (v. 46) Praise be to my Rock! Exalted be God my Saviour!

DAY 7 a) 1) The priests could not perform their duties, not even enter the temple. 2) All the Israelites knelt on the pavement, their faces to the ground, and worshipped giving thanks. Would we do that? 3) The king and the people gave sacrifices to the Lord.
b) Personal.

GUIDE TO STUDY 5

DAY 1 Beyond our understanding. His years past finding out. Beyond our reach. Unsearchable His judgements. His paths beyond tracing out.

DAY 2 a) God is holy.
b) He commands us to be holy.
c) He Himself makes us holy. This is a daily process for us to attain.

DAY 3 a) God is high, lofty, holy, and eternal. He also lives with those of a contrite heart.
b) He has promised to revive, heal, guide, restore, comfort and create praise and peace.

DAY 4 a) The paramount Lord of all, ruling, rewarding and judging. contrasts with the tender shepherd, tending, carrying and leading His flock.
b) *verse 12* – all-powerful, *verse 13* – incomprehensible, *verse 13-14* – all-knowing.

DAY 5 a) verse 22 – sovereign, verse 23 – omnipotent, verse 25 – God is incomparable. He is above everyone and every thing, verse 26 – magnificent creator and sustainer of all things.

b) Note Hebrews 1:2, 3, The Son is co-creator and co-sustainer of all things. Nothing is hidden from Him. He does not grow tired or weary (unchanging i.e. 'immutable'). sufficient.

DAY 6 verses 1-6, 15 – omnipotent, verses 7-12 – omnipresent, verses 13-16 – creator verses 14-16 – omniscient.

DAY 7 a) To keep us from falling. To present us before Him faultless, with great joy.

b) Jude Glory, majesty, power, authority. Holy, Lord God Almighty, worthy, our Lord and God, glory, honour, power.

It is on record that Martin Luther, at his first celebration of the Mass, was overcome by the realisation of the almightiness and majesty of God. In his own words he recalls that he was utterly stupefied and terror-stricken. He says, "With what tongue shall I address such majesty, seeing that all men ought to tremble at the presence of even an earthly prince? Who am I, that I should lift up my eyes or raise my hands to the Divine Majesty? The angels surround Him. At His nod the earth trembles. And shall I, a miserable little pygmy, say, 'I want this, I ask for that'? For I am dust and ashes and full of sin, and I am speaking to the living, eternal, and the true God."

Taken from 'The Holiness of God' by R.C. Sproul, Tyndale House Publishers Inc. Wheaton, Illinois, Sproul, quoting Roland Bainton, 'Here I Stand', NAL. 1978.

GUIDE TO STUDY 6

DAY 1 a) unchanging

b) Does not change, or lie, or change His mind. God is immutable. But, you say, we read that God does repent, or change His mind because of people's sin or their prayers. Within a great piece of machinery that is solid, and constant, there are nevertheless moving parts that make the whole a functional piece. God is solid, constant, and in that constancy, is able to 'change His mind' in response to man's response to Him.

DAY 2 a) His rulership is based on right decisions and judgements. He is unerringly just.

b) Personal. e.g. We would never be able to trust God to be fair. We would have no guidelines, stability, security, or objective standards.

DAY 3 a) He is faithful to His promises:
- calling us into fellowship with Jesus.
- in temptation we will not be given more than we can bear. He will make a way of escape for us. You may want to discuss some of the temptations we have and how God has enabled us to escape.- He forgives our sins, cleanses us completely.

b) God is utterly dependable, is perfect, just, faithful, upright. Through Jesus our Lord we may come to Him.

DAY 4 He has loved us with an everlasting love. He Himself has drawn us to Him – but within that drawing He has given us free choice to accept or reject His love, John 7:37, Revelation 22:17. He yearns over us, has great compassion for us. Are any among us yearning over a child, a husband? You are experiencing in a measure some of God's yearning.

DAY 5 Compassion, graciousness, slowness to anger, faithfulness, forgiveness, justice.

DAY 6 a) God is love. He loved us.
b) We have His Son as our atoning sacrifice for sins. We can therefore be born of God, live, can know God.
c) Discussion.

DAY 7 1) God is eternal, sovereign, holy, almighty. He has loved Jesus before the foundation of the world. Jesus was in God, was God. God is perfection. He cannot help but love perfection. He is Love!
2) Jesus has prayed that we might be with Him and see His Glory. Try to get the group to express how they will feel when they begin to comprehend what Jesus and His glory – and God's – is really like.

GUIDE TO STUDY 7

DAY 1 a) As Sovereign Lord
b) That God was King, in control, made the decisions, and that he, Abraham, was God's humble servant.

DAY 2 Abraham used the word LORD (Jehovah), giving God His own personal name.

DAY 3 a) *verse 13*; a ram, *verse 17*; descendants numerous as the stars and as the sand, *verse 18*; blessings for all nations.
b) Because Abraham obeyed.
c) Personal.

DAY 4 He was of the line of David. He reigned in life over all temptation, opposition and even the prince of this world, John 12:31; 14:30.
He was the only one who could be called Jehovah, John 8:58.
He is the only way we can become righteous.

DAY 5 a) Because God is holy. See also Genesis 1:27. God's original plan that man should be in God's image included holiness.
b) Yes, we may be holy because God makes us holy. In Christ we are made holy (set apart for God), sanctified and also we are commanded to practise holiness.

DAY 6 a) It was Jehovah who was protecting them, above them, before them, and was raised up as a banner recognised by the enemy.
b) 1) Jehovah is a stronghold, He is with me, He is my helper, I take refuge in Him.

2) I will look in triumph on my enemies. In the name of Jehovah I cut them off (3 times) It is the Lord's name that is the banner that creates fear and proclaims victory.

DAY 7 a) He knows us as individuals, provides, leads to good pasture, to water, protects, enfolds, comforts, tends wounds, leads us to a secure home.
b) Personal. The group may like to share their responses.

GUIDE TO STUDY 8

DAY 1 a) (v. 1-5) Was with God. Was God. Was in the beginning. Was co- creator of all things. Was source of life. Overcame darkness. (v. 14). Became human and lived among us. Displayed the glory of God.
b) Group discussion.
c) The glory of God was manifest and filled the tabernacle. So also the glory of God was manifest in Christ Jesus, filling Him.

DAY 2 a) Glory, grace, truth, mercy in redemption (v. 29), His eternity (v. 30).
b) Lamb of God who takes away the sin of the world. I saw the Spirit come down from heaven and remain on Him. He will baptise with the Holy Spirit. This is the Son of God.

DAY 3 a) The Most High. The Lord God. The Holy Spirit. The holy one. The Son of God.
b) Son of God. Jehovah the eternal self-existent one.

DAY 4 a) He: is heir of all things, made the universe, is the radiance of God's Glory; is the exact representation of God's being; sustains all things by His Word; has purified us from sin; is seated at the right hand of the majesty on high; is superior to all angels. The name (signifying His accomplishment) that He has inherited is superior to any name given to an angel. That name could be 'Redeemer', or 'The Lamb'. This Name, 'The Lamb', is the one given to Him throughout the book of Revelation.
b) Image – representation and manifestation, not merely a likeness. Image – exact, as of a wax seal.
(Matthew Henry has a good commentary on 'image'.)

DAY 5 a) Heaven opened, a dove, a voice from heaven. Face shone like the sun, clothes white as light, Moses and Elijah talking with Jesus, bright cloud, Voice from the cloud. Voice from heaven testifying that the Father had glorified His name.
b) Personal

DAY 6 The Son of Man – Jesus – is coming back in power and great Glory. We have referred very little to this great event in our studies, and it may be good here to allow the group to discuss it.

DAY 7 Be raised from the dead and ascend to heaven Be sovereign and head over the church, His body. Note that He fills everything, and His body the church, is His fullness! Wonderful divine mystery! Have the church displaying to heavenly rulers and authorities God's wisdom. We are God's show-window to principalities and powers both good and evil, displaying the might and wisdom of God in redeeming man back to Himself.

GUIDE TO STUDY 9

DAY 1 1) He was conceived by the overshadowing of the Holy Spirit.
2) He was announced by angels.
3) He was welcomed by Gentiles.
4) He was feared by the king.
5) He was blessed by a Spirit-led prophet.

DAY 2 a) Father-Son relationship.
b) He always addressed Him as Father. The only exception to this was when He was on the cross bearing the sin of the whole world. It appears also that in the O.T. only Jacob and Isaiah ever referred to God as their Father, but He was not in the O.T. addressed as Father.

DAY 3 Able to give life. Able to judge. Able to call the dead to life. Was before Abraham. Was God – Jehovah. Had completed the work God gave Him to do. You might want to make a challenge here – see Revelation 3:2

DAY 4 "I do nothing on my own but speak just as the Father taught me. Whatever I say is just what the Father has told me to say. I have come to do the will of Him who sent me." Challenge: Are we prepared to seek to emulate this?

DAY 5 The life of Christ is in us who believe in Him, that we are in Him and He in us. See 2 Peter 1:3.4. No-one else can claim to be the 'source of life'.

DAY 6 Scripture was fulfilled in detail:
The soldiers divided His garments among themselves by casting lots for them, Psalm 22:18. (If time permits you may wish to consider all of Ps. 22:1-24.)
– Jesus said, "I am thirsty", and vinegar was given Him to drink, Psalm 69:21.
– the soldiers pierced His side, Zechariah. 12:10.
– not one of His bones was broken, Psalm 34:20,
– the Passover Lamb was a picture of Christ
– He actively 'gave up His spirit'; John 19:30

DAY 7 a) He lives with you and will be in you. I will come to you. You will see me. I am in my Father, and you in me, and I in you. I will show myself to Him.
b) Personal e.g. If we believe in Christ we accept His life into ours. That life of His will flow out from us, in the way we live, speak, etc., giving life to others.

GUIDE TO STUDY 10

DAY 1 a) The Cross – Christ's death, burial and resurrection.
b) Because it is the only foundation and way to eternal life.
Through it there is a complete cut-off from the old life – the world.

DAY 2 Death, burial, resurrection of Jesus. Reconciliation with God. Not only were these the themes of the first sermons, but the theme of the whole of the New Testament. As we teach and minister to others, are we as clear-cut as to what the Gospel really is? Do we realise that the fulcrum of all of history and of eternity is the cross of Christ? The glory of God is the CROSS OF CHRIST.

DAY 3 "Your Will be done." "It is finished." "Rolled back the stone and sat on it." "He is risen."

DAY 4 1) Jesus shared our humanity. 2) Christ destroyed the devil, who held the power of death. You may need to discuss the fact that at the cross the devil's head was bruised, Genesis 3:15, Colossians 2:15, and even though he is still active today his power is broken and he is in subjection to the power of Christ. 3) Were made a new creation. 4) God reconciled us to Himself through Christ. 5) We have been given the ministry of reconciliation.

All N.T. teaching centres around these things. As we proclaim the death of Christ and the defeat of Satan we glorify God.

DAY 5 a) To bring us to Himself under one head – Christ.
b) By His love, His grace, His mercy He saved us and lifted us into heavenly realms in Christ Jesus. Here we have an on-going place in Him (Col. 3:3) throughout our lives and on into eternity.
c) Personal. e.g. It is through Jesus Christ that we are able to be presented before God's glorious presence without fault and with great joy.

DAY 6 a) Jesus was crucified, slain for people of every ethnic group in the world. People from all groups are made into one kingdom, and a priesthood to reign on the earth.
b) He is at the centre of the throne, absolute ruler over all, and the focus of the worship of myriads of angels and heavenly hosts.

DAY 7 a) The marriage of the church to the Lamb, the crucified Jesus. If it is suitable to your group you may wish to follow this up in 21:1-4, pointing out 'new earth', 'new heaven', 'new Jerusalem', and that the new Jerusalem is the bride, the church, 9-11. See also 22:1-5.
b) He is the Temple (centre of worship) the lamp (the holder of Glory), the source of life, and supreme ruler.

GUIDE TO STUDY 11

DAY 1 We are chosen by God, a royal family; a priesthood – able to minister to God and on behalf of others; we belong to God, have received mercy. As we know Him we have all we need for life and godliness.
We have great and precious promises so that we may participate in the divine nature! – and escape the corruption of the world.

DAY 2 a) Believe. Receive Him.
b) 1) We are sons of God, can call Him "Father". 2) We have the Holy Spirit within. 3) We are heirs of God and joint-heirs with Christ. 4) We share His Glory! 5) We are free. 6) We reflect the Lord's Glory. 7) We are being transformed into His likeness.

DAY 3 e.g. verse 10 Glory has come to Jesus through His disciples. verses 20-26 Jesus prayed for us also. He prayed that we should be one – not only unity but union; not an organisation but a single organism. He has shared the life of the Father and the Son with us; we share His Glory; we share the love the Father has for the Son. This love flows through us to each other, and is the testimony to the world that we are His disciples John 13:34-35.

DAY 4 a) Knowing God, as we see Him and His glory in Jesus.
b) He has given us His Holy Spirit, and by this we are able to understand. The Holy Spirit searches into the deep things of God, and reveals them to us, thus bringing glory to Jesus. These things are not taught and cannot be taught by human wisdom. It is impossible for a person without the Holy Spirit to understand them.
c) Personal

DAY 5 a) There are different members with different functions, each one necessary to the whole. Note v.18. What justification do we have to belittle any person because of how he is made or what he cannot do?
b) Teaching. Fellowship. Prayer. Hospitality and the Lord's Supper. Sharing goods. Increase in numbers.

DAY 6 The many-sided wisdom of God is displayed to rulers and authorities in heavenly realms as they see the church and how it came into being.
We reflect the Lord's glory, being increasingly changed into His likeness. We shine like stars in the universe.

DAY 7 a) Suffering and glory.
b) Rejoice, because we share the suffering of Christ. Realise we are blessed because the Spirit of glory and of God rests on us.
Praise God, because we bear His name.

GUIDE TO STUDY 12

DAY 1 1) He reigns, is majestic, is strong, is mightier than pounding seas; He has reigned from all eternity; He is holy; His commandments are unchanging; all Heaven and earth are not sufficient to contain Him; He is worthy to receive glory and honour and power.

2) He created and established the world, and all things in it.

DAY 2 a) The Lion of the tribe of Judah, the Root of David, the Lamb.

b) He has been slain and has purchased by His death people from every tribe, language and nation.

DAY 3 a) Hunger (famine), thirst (drought), no shelter (evicted, refugees), suffering and tears.

b) They were cleansed from sin, knew Christ as Saviour.

c) e.g. for fortitude, faith in God, joy in Christ. hope, courage, endurance to the end. That they may have an unblemished testimony.

DAY 4 a) e.g. by reminding us again of sins that have been forgiven; by telling us we are of no value; making us worry instead of handing the matter over to God.

b) By the Blood of the Lamb, i.e. trust in Christ for salvation, for ongoing forgiveness of sin, 1 John 1:9. Remembering that Christ came to destroy the works of the devil (1 John 3:8) and He has destroyed him (Col. 2:15), and we are above, safely hidden with Christ in God (Col. 3:2, 3). By the word of our testimony – being bold in declaring God's power and His victory. By focusing on Jesus rather than on our problem.

DAY 5 a) The saints, God's people, His true church.

b) Personal. e.g. God and His people dwelling together; all things new; being able to drink freely from the water of life; will inherit all things; the Lord God and the Lamb are the temple – unhindered worship; glory of God is its light; nothing impure will ever enter it.

DAY 6 a) Lord God Almighty, and the Lamb (Christ); the glory of God;

b) the Lamb;

c) Life; the throne of God and the Lamb, life comes from Him.

d) Everlasting.

DAY 7 a) By completing the work God gave Him to do, redeeming us from sin.

b) That we are with Him and see His glory.

c) God has called us to His eternal glory through the life, death and resurrection of our Lord Jesus Christ. After we have suffered a little while we will enjoy His eternal glory. How can we ever praise Him enough?

GEARED FOR GROWTH BIBLE STUDIES

Enable you to:

1. Have a daily encounter with God
2. Encourage you to apply the Word of God to everyday life
3. Help you to share your faith with others
4. They are straightforward, practical, non-controversial and inexpensive.

WEC INTERNATIONAL is involved in gospel outreach, church planting and discipleship training using every possible means including radio, literature, medical work, rural development schemes, correspondence courses and telephone counselling. Nearly two thousand workers are involved in their fields and sending bases.

Find out more from the following Website:
www.wec-int.org.uk

A full list of over 50 'Geared for Growth' studies can be obtained from:

UK GEARED FOR GROWTH COORDINATORS
　　　John and Ann Edwards
　　　8, Sidings Terrace, Skewen, Neath, West Glamorgan SA10 6RE
　　　Email: rhysjohn.edwards@virgin.net
　　　Tel. 01792 814994

UK Website: www.gearedforgrowth.co.uk

For information on Geared for Growth Bible Studies in other languages contact:

Word Worldwide International Coordinators
Kip and Doreen Wear
Tel. 01269 870842
Email: kip.wear@virgin.net

Christian Focus Publications
Publishes books for all ages

Our mission statement –
STAYING FAITHFUL
In dependence upon God we seek to help make His infallible word, the Bible, relevant. Our aim is to ensure that the Lord Jesus Christ is presented as the only hope to obtain forgiveness of sin, live a useful life and look forward to heaven with Him.
REACHING OUT
Christ's last command requires us to reach out to our world with His gospel. We seek to help fulfil that by publishing books that point people towards Jesus and help them to develop a Christ-like maturity. We aim to equip all levels of readers for life, work, ministry and mission.

Books in our adult range are published in three imprints.
Christian Focus contains popular works including biographies, commentaries, basic doctrine, and Christian living. Our children's books are published in this imprint.
Mentor focuses on books written at a level suitable for Bible College and seminary students, pastors, and other serious readers. The imprint includes commentaries, doctrinal studies, examination of current issues, and church history.
Christian Heritage contains classic writings from the past.

For details of our titles visit us on our website
www.christianfocus.com

ISBN 978-1-84550-410-6
Copyright © WEC International
Published in 2008
by
Christian Focus Publications,
Geanies House, Fearn, Ross-shire,
IV20 1TW, Scotland
and
WEC International, Bulstrode,
Oxford Road, Gerrards Cross, Bucks, SL9 8SZ

Cover design by Alister MacInnes
Printed Bell & Bain, Glasgow